SCOTLAND

LANDMARKS, LANDSCAPES & HIDDEN TREASURES

Publisher and Creative Director: Nick Wells
Picture Research and Editoral: Josie Mitchell
Project Editor: Cat Taylor
Art Director: Mike Spender
Digital Design and Production: Chris Herbert

Special thanks to: Frances Bodiam, Sarah Goulding, Amanda Leigh,
Victoria Lyle, Melinda Révèsz, Gemma Walters and Polly Prior

FLAME TREE PUBLISHING
Crabtree Hall, Crabtree Lane
Fulham, London SW6 6TY
United Kingdom

www.flametreepublishing.com

First published 2015

19 17 15 16 18
1 3 5 7 9 10 8 6 4 2

A CIP record for this book is available from the British Library.

ISBN: 978 1 78361 422 6

Printed in Singapore

SCOTLAND

LANDMARKS, LANDSCAPES & HIDDEN TREASURES

Text by Michael Kerrigan

FLAME TREE
PUBLISHING

Contents

Introduction

"When I am asked about Scotland how did I like it, my enthusiasm for it makes people repent of their question and I must remember that I am in England which is jealous of the land of the mountain and the flood."

Krystyn Lach-Syrma spent over three years in Scotland, from 1820, with the two Polish princes to whom he was tutor. The country was enjoying something of a 'Golden Age' just then: the visitor met Sir Walter Scott, James Hogg and other luminaries – his royal pupils were a passport to the most fashionable soirées and the stateliest homes. In 1824, he headed south with his young charges for a season in London, but his letter to a friend in Scotland makes clear just how profound an impression the country had made on him. Was the remark about English "jealousy" justified? We can only wonder: what is clear is how strong a proxy-patriot he had become. He was not the first foreign visitor to fall in love with Scotland, of course; he would certainly not be the last.

Where he differs from many more recent visitors, however, is in the breadth of his affections: it was as much as anything the variety of the Scottish scene that stirred his soul. *From Charlotte Square to Fingal's Cave* (tr. Helena Brochowska, ed. Mona McLeod, 2004) is the memoir of the time he spent in Scotland. Intelligent and insightful as it frequently is, what is striking to the reader today is his receptiveness to the variety of what the country had to offer. Though Scotland was to him (in Burns's phrase) "the land of the mountain and the flood", it was also the land of the factory and the canal. He was as susceptible as any

romantic visitor to the grandeur of a Highland glen, but he could appreciate a classical façade or ornamental shrubbery too. He thrilled to hear tales of kilted cattle-raiders but admired the industry and ingenuity of the Lowland farmer, and revered the scholars of Scotland's medieval universities. He loved the writings of Walter Scott, but was every bit as excited at the cutting-edge researches of Scottish scientists and the new industries which technology had opened the way to.

It is in just this spirit that this book sets out to reveal the full diversity of the Scottish scene. Dennis Hardley has explored the remotest reaches of the Highlands and Islands to find vistas of heartstopping sublimity and haunting atmosphere. A lyrical poet with the camera, he reminds us once again of the exhilarating beauty of a country whose wild ruggedness has caught the imagination of the world. But he captures another country, too: some of the best-kept secrets, famously, are hidden in open view, and Hardley finds fresh inspiration in less obviously

dramatic settings. Here are winding rivers, rolling fields, orderly parklands, neat little textile towns and magnificent mansions – not to mention the busy streets and squares of modern cities.

For the sake of convenience and clarity, this book divides the country into separate regions. Necessarily, these divisions are – to some degree – arbitrary. Yet there are clear distinctions between the different parts of Scotland – not only in geology, landscape and geographical situation, but in their often vastly dissimilar experiences over several thousand years. The Western Isles, which for several centuries history tied more closely to Scandinavia than to Scotland, have developed a special character all their own. As time went on a Gaelic tradition would emerge, linking Lewis, Harris and the other outer Isles more closely with the Northern Highlands: the counties of Caithness, Sutherland, Ross and Cromarty, the region we move on to consider next. The Southern Highlands, as covered here, embraces the area to the south of Inverness and includes Strathspey and Nairn as well as Lochaber and Lochalsh. In geological and scenic terms, the Inner Hebrides (Skye, Mull, Islay, Colonsay and many more) can be seen as continuations of the Southern Highlands, but their history – and of course their island culture – sets them apart. To the east of the Highlands proper sprawl the Grampians, just as mountainous at their centre but sloping down to the gentler country of the coast. Tucked-away fishing villages line the North Sea shoreline – largely unknown to the outsider; here too is the 'Granite City', Aberdeen. There are more cities to the south in central Scotland, notably Dundee, Perth and Stirling – but also some of the country's most spectacular scenes. The 'Lowlands' begin here, but as this and succeeding chapters show, landscapes in this region are often hilly by any normal standards.

Around the Firth of Forth is to be found the heart of historic Scotland: the cathedral and castle at St Andrews, the palace at Linlithgow and, of course, Edinburgh. Yet history plays strange tricks: through much of the first millennium AD, the Lothians formed part of the Anglo-Saxon kingdom of Northumbria. Edinburgh, a Celtic hillfort, was a hotly contested site. Pulled back and forth between Picts and Angles, it finally fell to the former, but Scotland's future capital had come within a whisker of being an 'English' city. Not that Scotland as we know it existed yet: much of the next region, the area now covered by Glasgow, the Clyde Valley and Argyll, belonged (with the inshore islands) to the Celtic kingdom of Dál Riata. This was essentially an Irish realm, the Glens of Antrim its originating centre; the North Channel functioned not as a frontier but as a connecting link. It may seem strange from a modern standpoint, but with such difficult terrain to the landward side, this part of Scotland naturally looked westward out to sea.

It just goes to show how misleading simplistic notions of 'Scottishness' may be, a fact only underlined when we come to consider the southwest. Just across the border from England lies one of Scotland's least-known regions, a place apart even in the Scottish scheme of things. From its wild hills to its isolated farmsteads, Galloway gives the impression of being out on a geographical and cultural limb; even Ayrshire feels aloof from the country as a whole.

To the east, Dumfries gives on to the contested territory of the Borders, a region formed by several centuries of incessant conflict. Its identity ambivalent, it defined itself against the England with which its inhabitants were so much of the time at war – but in doing so it set itself apart to a certain extent from the rest of Scotland.

In the end, though, it has to be faced that if there is one single thing that binds Scotland together as a nation, it is the age-old rivalry – long an actual enmity – with England. That is clear in what is widely seen as the country's founding document, the Declaration of Arbroath, which was signed by the Scottish lords in 1320. If Robert the Bruce sold Scotland out to England, they warned,

"… we should exert ourselves at once to drive him out as our enemy and a subverter of his own rights and ours, and make some other man who was well able to defend us our King; for, as long as but a hundred of us remain alive, never will we on any conditions be brought under English rule."

Brave words, which many Scots felt had to be eaten after the Union of the Parliaments in 1707, though this would, in theory, be a marriage of equal partners rather than an act of domination. Though staged specifically in support of the claims of the House of Stewart to rule in Britain as a whole, the Jacobite rebellions of 1715 and 1745 have often been seen as being broadly nationalistic in their inspiration. But Scottish opinion was bitterly divided on these uprisings, and Scots made up the bulk of the armies that quelled them: many were strongly in favour of the Union.

In part this was because Presbyterian Scots felt more in common with a Protestant England than they did with the Catholic-leaning Stewarts and their continental allies. Scots 'Covenanters' in the seventeenth century had rebelled against Stewart England on religious grounds; now the same loyalties drew many to set aside the national enmities of old. The Reformation made its unmistakeable mark on Scotland: Protestantism would prove an important aspect of the identity of the modern Scot, who was stereotypically dour. Even here, though, it is dangerous to generalize: parts of the Highlands and Islands remained resolutely Catholic, whilst the nineteenth century saw Catholic immigrants streaming in from famine-stricken Ireland to the Lowland cities.

Subsequent waves of immigration from southern and eastern Europe, the Indian subcontinent and other parts of the world have seen the emergence of a modern multicultural society in Scotland. As elsewhere, that has not been without its challenges. Historically, however, Scotland has been a country in which different cultures, apparently ill-suited, have been able to come together in a common patriotic cause.

Western Isles

The Western Isles are a place apart, not so much the Outer Hebrides as the Outer Darkness as far as generations of English – and even Scots – have been concerned.

That alien quality is by no means entirely imaginary – these islands were ruled by the Kings of Norway until well into the thirteenth century and, since then, the Gaelic tongue has been spoken here. Yet the 'Long Island' of Lewis and Harris and its southward-straggling tail of smaller islands (North Uist, Benbecula, South Uist, Barra and Mingulay) can claim to be the oldest region of the British Isles. Britain's most ancient rock strata are found here, formed some

2,700 million years ago, along with some of the earliest signs of human settlement, from around 4000 BC. Today, scattered ruins remain – in particular those standing stones which, though clear signs of human presence, merely underline the eerie emptiness of the Hebridean landscape.

Lashed by Atlantic storms for much of the year, far removed from centres of modernity, the Outer Hebrides have a distinctly forgotten feel. But by the same token they are utterly unspoiled; their beauty, though sometimes austere, is often breathtaking, and when the sun comes out there is no more exquisite spot on earth.

Tolsta Head
ISLE OF LEWIS

Right. A bright and breezy Hebridean day sets the clouds scudding across an endless sky; white horses canter in at a lively clip along a sandy beach. Often, though, the winds are wilder far, blowing horizontal rain across the scene and battering the coast with crashing breakers. On days like that, the cliffs around Tolsta Head – the most exhilarating of walks in fine conditions – become a death-trap for the unwary walker. Towering waves assail these rocky heights and storm-blasts whip in with extraordinary force: you could easily be swept into the sea.

Harbour and Town
STORNOWAY, ISLE OF LEWIS

Next page. A Mediterranean sun lights up Stornoway and its lovely natural harbour, belying the Western Isles' reputation for barrenness. "On the contrary," wrote Dean Monro, a cleric who came here in 1549, Lewis was "fair and well inhabited at the coast, fertile and fruitful." The Outer Hebrides' only significant town, Stornoway has weathered economic turbulence of late, with downturns in tweedmaking and the vital herring fishery. But these blows have been cushioned by the rise of the tourist industry: Stornoway today is a thriving regional capital.

Stone Circle
CALLANISH, ISLE OF LEWIS

Right. A visit to the stone circle at Callanish is a truly unforgettable experience: stand here and look, and feel the millennia melt away. Babylon was not built when ancient masons started raising these megaliths 5,000 years ago, but this gusty promontory above Loch Roag probably looked much the same as it does now. Much is still to be discovered about the lives of Lewis's first human inhabitants, but there is widespread evidence of settlement dating back to the earliest Neolithic times.

Towards the North Harris Hills
LUSKENTYRE, SOUTH HARRIS

Next page. The afterglow of a smouldering sundown sets sea and sky ablaze, a dramatic frame for this splendid view of the North Harris hills. In the foreground, waves wash the mudflats just offshore at Luskentyre; beyond lie the deeper waters of the Sound of Taransay. It is a ravishing sight and, in this modern age, an exceptional one: no man-made interference disrupts the symphonic play of natural light. No sodium streetlamp glare, no headlights, no shop signs are to be seen; not even the merest glint from a cottage window.

Leverburgh
SOUTH HARRIS

Right. As recently as 1921 this little township in southern Harris was known as Obbe: it was renamed in honour of Lord Leverhulme, who had bought both Lewis and Harris. The wealthy manufacturer of Sunlight Soap was also a dreamer-up of ambitious social schemes – he planned to make this the productive centre serving his nationwide fishmongers' chain 'MacFisheries'. Like so many before him, Leverhulme ran up against the islanders' independent spirit. He gave up and moved on, his only legacy his name.

St Clement's Church
RODEL, SOUTH HARRIS

Next page. There is believed to have been a church at Rodel for several centuries. Visiting Harris in 1549, Dean Monro noted "a monastery with a steeple". The structure he saw is thought to have been newly built – though completed just in time, as it turned out – to have its function abolished by the Scottish Reformation. Far removed from ecclesiastical oversight, Catholicism clung on in a number of the Western Isles, but those that converted (including Harris) adopted an especially ferocious form of Protestantism.

Castlebay
ISLE OF BARRA

Right. Ferries are the mainstay of island life in Castlebay Harbour, Barra. The 'Cal Mac' (Caledonian MacBrayne) is the main source of transportation. Carrying passengers, post, cars and freight of every kind, they ply back and forth daily linking 22 different Hebridean isles in total, and provide an essential connection with the mainland. On the hillside above the harbour stands the Church of Our Lady, Star of the Sea. Barra is one of those islands whose people remained Catholic despite the Reformation.

Traigh Mhor Beach
ISLE OF BARRA

Next page. Traigh Mhor Beach on the northeastern side of Barra has for centuries been celebrated for its cockles; more recently it has doubled as a landing strip. The famous writer, Compton Mackenzie, built a bungalow above this beach in 1934, where he wrote many of his most famous works including the classic comic novel *Whisky Galore* (1947). He based his story on an actual incident, the foundering of the whisky-laden SS *Politician*, which was wrecked at Calvay, just off the neighbouring island of Eriksay, in 1941.

Northern Highlands

There are parts of the northern Highlands where you can walk all day without finding a road; before the eighteenth century you could have gone a week or more.

That was when General Wade set about building his network of military roads – part of the pacification programme for a seditious and unruly region. Here, the House of Hanover knew, the people's first loyalty lay not with their official monarchy but with their clan chieftains; their second, often as not, with the Stewarts 'across the water'.

Today the tumults are long gone, though there is a melancholy edge to the prevailing peace and quiet. As elsewhere in the Highlands, the 'unspoiled' character is not

entirely natural. Shamefully sold out by their chiefs, thousands of the rural poor were forced off their smallholdings in the 'Clearances' of the nineteenth century to make way for more lucrative sheep-farming.

Oddly, the northernmost part of the region, Caithness, is the gentlest when it comes to scenery, its green fields contrasting starkly with Sutherland's wild mountains and desolate moors. Wester Ross has some of Scotland's most stunning upland views, and the entire northwest coast is one of the scenic wonders of the British Isles.

Yesnaby Sea Stack
ORKNEY

Right. At once exquisite and unimaginably massive, a slender needle of solid rock, this stack was whittled away over countless centuries by the eternal to-ing and fro-ing of the ocean waves. It stands just off Mainland, Orkney, on a stretch of coastline punctuated by similar formations, a playground for rock climbers in recent decades. This stack rises sheer to a height of 35 m (115 ft): it is not considered to be particularly challenging by serious climbers – though the first known ascent was not made until 1967.

Kirkwall Harbour
ORKNEY

Next page. Fishing boats line the basin of what remains a bustling port, with ferries to Aberdeen and Lerwick as well as to the other Orkney islands. Kirkwall is the capital not just of Mainland but of the whole island group: its history dates back the best part of 1,000 years. It warranted a mention in the Orkneyinga Saga – which scholars date to the year 1046 – though it was almost certainly settled some time before. Then too it was a port, a stopping-off point for traders (and raiders) making their way to Britain, Ireland and points west.

Sinclair and Girnigoe Castle
WICK, CAITHNESS

Right. Another stronghold of the Sinclair family, this twofold fortress stands on Noss Head, just north of Wick, Caithness; Girnigoe Castle, the original structure, dates from around 1480. The more elegant and commodious Sinclair Castle was built a little way inland in 1606. Since this contained the family's living quarters, it bore the brunt of the cannonade when the Clan Campbell came calling in 1690. It is ironic, then, that the medieval section is in better repair than its more modern counterpart, but an ambitious scheme is under way with hopes of restoring both.

Noss Head Lighthouse
WICK, CAITHNESS

Next page. A perfect blue sea stretches away to the horizon, and Noss Head lighthouse stands tall in the foreground. Though the northernmost district of the Highlands, Caithness has a Lowland character, with its largely level plains and fertile soils. To seaward it is rather less welcoming, though – hence the need for the Noss Head light to guide shipping safely past one of Scotland's most treacherous, rockbound coasts.

Dunrobin Castle
GOLSPIE, CAITHNESS

Right. Dunrobin Castle is more a château than a castle in the conventional sense. It was actually built around a genuine medieval core, laid down in 1275 by Robert, Earl of Sutherland, on a strategic sea-coast site north of Golspie in Caithness. No sign of that can be seen in the structure as re-imagined in the 1840s by Sir Charles Barry, architect of the Palace of Westminster, however. An extravagant Gothic confection, with spacious ornamental grounds extending landward, it was conceived with gracious living rather than defence in mind.

Stac Polly
INVERPOLLY, SUTHERLAND

Next page. Occasionally picturesque, the Northern Highlands are often awesomely spectacular, but sometimes they are eerily primeval in their beauty. Here Stac Polly rises high above the placid waters of Loch Lurgain in a scene that cannot have changed much over several million years. Up close, Stac Polly looks very different, countless centuries of wind and weather having eroded its soft sandstone into myriad exotic forms. It has become an adventure playground for climbers, who congregate here each weekend to explore its jagged outcrops and tackle its dizzying pinnacles.

Eilean Donan Castle
LOCH DUICH, ROSS-SHIRE

Right. The castle was rebuilt in the early twentieth century, with scant regard for historical accuracy, but Scotland's most photographed fortress is no mere folly. In fact, its story is as romantic as its setting. Built in the fourteenth century (the surrounding wall is even older), the family seat of the Mackenzies became one of the bases for the Jacobite rising of 1719. A Spanish garrison sat helplessly here whilst the warships of the Crown reduced the walls to rubble all around them.

Mam Ratagan Pass
ROSS-SHIRE

Next page. Mam Ratagan was once the main route across the western hills for drovers herding livestock to the markets of the Lowlands. The scenery is stunning, but it is safe to assume this was wasted on cattle thoroughly traumatized after the enforced swim over the sea from Skye. Today's tourist can, however, appreciate the view across Loch Duich to the peaks of Kintail, said to have been five forsaken brides – a local chieftain's daughters – turned to stone out of pity by a sorcerer's spell.

Port of Ullapool
WESTER ROSS

Right. Ullapool occupies the only significant stretch of level ground to be found around the rugged shores of Loch Broom in Wester Ross, with its name believed to have derived from its foundation by a Norseman named 'Olaf'. The railway never quite made it here, despite the passing of an Act of Parliament (1890) authorising construction, but this has remained the major port for ferries to the outer isles. It is now a major tourist centre, the perfect holiday base for anybody wishing to explore the northern Highlands.

Loch Maree
WESTER ROSS

Next page. Solitary pines stand sentinel above the waters of Loch Maree in Wester Ross, with Ben Slioch rising in the distance and clouds that seem to curdle an ethereal azure sky. The whole scene might have been dreamed into existence as a landscape fit for a mythical hero to make his way across en route to some fateful encounter with his destiny. The Highland terrain itself is acknowledged to offer some of the finest scenery in the world: add in the Highland light and we have something almost spectral, otherworldly.

Falls of Rogie

EASTER ROSS

Right. Deep in the Torrachilty Forest, a couple of miles to the west of Contin, Easter Ross, the Black Water River thunders over the Falls of Rogie. Although a splendid sight for the spellbound visitor, it represents a serious obstacle for the salmon which have to make their way upstream to reach their ancestral spawning grounds each year. Remarkably, many succeed in making the leap – an extraordinary feat of animal athleticism. For those who fail, a salmon ladder has now been built alongside the waterfall.

Southern Highlands

From Nairn, south through Strathspey and Lochaber, lies some of Scotland's most spectacular scenery, and westward across the Great Glen is even more.

Ben Nevis, Britain's highest peak, is here, though at only 1,344 m (4,408 ft) it would scarcely qualify as a hill in any of the truly mountainous regions of the world. But then that is arguably what makes the Scottish Highlands so special: they offer sublimity on a human scale.

A sense of human history always haunts the visitor here. Every mountain, every glen, every pass has its own story. Old battlefields; ruined castles; the abandoned cottages of the

Clearances: the memories of past tragedies are a living presence in the landscape. A stunning setting by any standards, Glencoe undoubtedly has an extra resonance thanks to a consciousness of the terrible deeds done here three centuries ago. The Highland scene is not merely beautiful but romantic, a stage on which great and terrible dramas have been enacted.

Yet, if the melancholy minor key is always present, it is hard to stay sombre for long: the sheer loveliness of the landscape is exhilarating. A sudden burst of sunshine, a bend in the road presenting a new vista – wherever one goes, there is something fresh and delightful to be seen.

Greig Street Bridge
INVERNESS

Right. The Greig Street suspension bridge spans the fast-flowing River Ness, and was completed in 1881. The great German novelist Theodor Fontane observed, when he visited the town in the 1850s, that Inverness always was "a forward-thrusting town". Though often patronized by outsiders, who assume it to be a sleepy backwater, the 'capital of the Highlands' has always been remarkable for its liveliness and energy. Since the millennium it has been – by royal appointment – not a town but a city, looking forward optimistically to the future.

Urquhart Castle
LOCH NESS, INVERNESS-SHIRE

Next page. On a little promontory of land jutting out into Loch Ness stands the ancient fortress known as Urquhart Castle. There was a fort here in the Iron Age; the first 'modern' castle dates from the twelfth century but it has been razed and rebuilt several times in the centuries since. England's Edward I, 'Hammer of the Scots', seized it in 1296 and again in 1308 – Robert I of Scotland retook it that same year. It went on to feature in the rebellions of both the Covenanters and Jacobites.

Glenfinnan Kirk
INVERNESS-SHIRE

Right. Spring explodes in the Highlands like a sigh of relief after the long, dark months of winter. Green leaves break forth, flowers burst into bloom and cotton-wool clouds scud across the sky, as though nature is trying its best to make up for lost time. St Mary and St Finnan's Catholic Church, Glenfinnan, is perfectly placed to enjoy the show, with stupendous views across Loch Shiel. St Finnan, an early Irish missionary, is said to have had a hermit's cell on an island in the loch.

Glencoe
INVERNESS-SHIRE

Next page. A hiker takes time out amidst the splendours of Glencoe. The southern Highlands are perfectly suited to hill-walking and climbing. Every grade of walk is to be had, from decorous stroll to serious mountaineering – many routes, of course, change their character with the season. Winter walking is a specialized pursuit, to be undertaken only by the experienced, and even then with careful preparation. Even in summer, the Highlands must be treated with respect: sudden storms may blow up out of nowhere, and disorientating mists can descend when least expected.

Fort William and Loch Linnhe
INVERNESS-SHIRE

Right. General Monck of Cromwell's Commonwealth army built a fort near here in 1654 as part of his wider plan to bring an unco-operative Scotland under control. It was rebuilt, reinforced and re-christened 'Fort William' in 1690, when the unseating of the Stewarts had set the Highlands seething. One of the biggest of the sea lochs, Loch Linnhe was not formed by glacial action like most of the others, but marks the southern end of that great geological fault which cleaves the Highlands down the middle.

Loch Leven
INVERNESS-SHIRE

Next page. Loch Leven is the looking-glass for this extraordinary image, its still waters reflecting the Mamore Hills and Glencoe village. A study in symmetry, it captures all the peace and tranquillity of a winter's day in which no sound breaks the silence, no ripple interrupts the water's surface. A branch of Loch Linnhe, narrow at the mouth, and crowded round by mountains on every side, Loch Leven is sheltered from the worst of the weather, its waters always comparatively calm.

Ruthven Barracks
KINGUSSIE, STRATHSPEY

Right. The notorious fourteenth-century warlord, the Wolf of Badenoch, had his stronghold on this rise which controls comings and goings along the vital valley of Strathspey. After the Jacobite rising of 1715, Crown forces built a barracks, only to have it seized by the rebels in the course of the ''45'. The Jacobite survivors of Culloden holed up here to lick their wounds, and before dispersing, they blew it up to keep it out of government hands. So it still stands, a broken monument to shattered hopes and dreams.

Rannoch Moor
RANNOCH

Next page. "Here the crow starves," wrote T.S. Eliot, "…here the patient stag / Breeds for the rifle. Between the soft moor / And the soft sky, scarcely room / To leap or soar." There is an eerie otherworldliness about Rannoch even in the sunniest summer weather; in deep winter there is no bleaker place on earth.

Glen Nevis
LOCHABER

Right. Sunshine and fresh snow, a ravishing combination in any Highland setting, lends a wonderful jewelled beauty to this Lochaber scene. Beyond the frosty scene spreads the exquisite tracery of the trees. A deep, steep-sided valley gouged out by glaciers in successive ice ages, Glen Nevis skirts the southwestern edge of the Ben Nevis range. Britain's highest summit is covered with snow for much of the year.

Corpach Basin
LOCHABER

Next page. Corpach marks the western end of the Great Glen, and the entrance to the Caledonian Canal which runs through the heart of the Highlands to emerge into the Moray Firth outside Inverness. Famous as the father of the steam engine, James Watt originally surveyed the course for this waterway, with construction undertaken by another distinguished engineer, Thomas Telford. But, heroic as their achievements were, they are dwarfed by those of nature, as exemplified by the brooding mass of Ben Nevis beyond Loch Linnhe.

Highland Cow
WESTERN HIGHLANDS

Right. She may look a little grotesque beside the sleeker breeds that one is used to seeing, but the Highland cow is perfectly adapted to her Highland setting. Far from impeding vision, the long fringe helps protect the eyes from flies and parasites and the shaggy coat keeps out the searing cold, the biting winds and squalls of snow and rain. Despite her impressive horns she has an exceptionally placid disposition, while her stocky build gives her toughness: Highland cattle are strongly resistant to disease. Low birth-weight makes calving less complicated and more safe.

INNER ISLANDS

"Well, here we are in Skye, and it feels like the South Seas" wrote the English novelist Virginia Woolf to her sister in 1938. It was not just the fact of being surrounded by sea, or her sense of remoteness from the railways and the London papers, but the almost mystic atmosphere, the eerie translucence of the air. "Hardly embodied,' she elaborated, in a postcard to a friend: 'Like living in a jellyfish lit up with green light."

Countless other visitors to the Inner Hebrides have experienced the same sense of strangeness, that trick of the light which lends a special resonance to every scene.

Many seasoned Hebridean travellers insist that the Hebridean light varies considerably from isle to isle: Mull and Islay, they say, differ as much as Colonsay does from Kerrera. Others point more sceptically to the enormous variety of the islands in geological origins, landscape and history – naturally, each one has a different 'feel'.

What can hardly be disputed is the extraordinary beauty of the Inner Hebrides, and the remarkable variety of scenery they present. There are scores of islands here, each with its own distinctive character. You could explore them for years without ever exhausting their variety.

Storr Rock
TROTTERNISH, ISLE OF SKYE

Right. The tallest of these basalt pinnacles is known as 'the Old Man of Storr' which, despite looking like a man-made megalith, was formed naturally. Countless millennia of wind and rain wore away the softer rock around it, while other formations, every bit as strange, lie all around. Just across the Trotternish peninsula to westward, on the shores of Loch Kensaleyre, is a cluster of stones that really does seem to have been erected by humans. Legend has it that it was the tripod for a giant's cooking cauldron.

Towards the Cuillins
GESTO BAY, ISLE OF SKYE

Next page. "Rising on the other side of sorrow", in the stirring words of Skye's most famous modern Gaelic poet, Sorley Maclean, the Cuillin Hills form a dramatic backdrop to this view of Skye. Literally, in this case, they rise on the other side of Loch Harport, as much a challenge to climbers as an inspiration to poets. Gaelic tradition holds that the Cuillins were named after the Irish hero Cuchulain, but scholars suggest a less colourful etymology – from 'Kjöllen', an Old Norse word meaning 'keel-shaped ridges'.

Elgol Pier
ISLE OF SKYE

Right. Elgol lies in southwestern Skye, on the shores of Loch Skavaig. The jetty here was built in the 1990s for the shipping of marble quarried nearby, but by attracting pleasure craft it has also helped boost the tourist trade. Across the loch to the left can be seen the eastern edge of the Isle of Soay; beyond looms the jagged mass of the Cuillin Hills. Though some distance from the southern Cuillins, Elgol is as close as any real road gets, so it has become an important base for their exploration.

Towards the Cuillins
LOCH EISHORT, ISLE OF SKYE

Next page. Looking out from the northern shore of the Sleat Peninsula, this panoramic prospect of the sunset across Gauskavaig Bay and Loch Eishort is dominated by the distant forms of the Cuillins. Closer to hand, at the end of the rocky headland, there is the massive stack on which Dunsgaith Castle squats. This was the home of the MacDonalds until the sixteenth century and, though little of the ruin actually remains, the natural fortifications are formidable enough.

Dunvegan Castle
ISLE OF SKYE

Right. The chiefs of the Clan Macleod have made their homes here since the twelfth century, though much of the present structure dates from the sixteenth. It was a perfect situation: Dunvegan Loch offered a superbly sheltered anchorage – for a long time, indeed, the castle could only be entered from the sea. The 'fairy flag' kept here is said to have been given to a Macleod by his fairy lover many centuries since. It was to be waved in the time of the clan's direst adversity when it would summon supernatural assistance.

Morar Sands
RUM AND EIGG

Next page. Scotland's light is justly famous – they say it is very different on the country's eastern and western sides, but nowhere is it more exhilarating than on the little stretch of coast extending north from Arisaig. Here, beneath an azure sky, the Silver Sands of Morar give the sea a note of tropic turquoise – more South Pacific than western Inverness-shire. Rising up in the distance we see the islands of Rum and Eigg; along with Canna and Muck they are the largest of the so-called 'Small Isles', which help to shelter this section of the coast.

Towards Ben More
LOCH NA KEAL, ISLE OF MULL

Right. Looking southward across the loch, the mass of Ben More dominates the skyline: at 966 m (3,169 ft) it is Mull's highest mountain. It is, indeed, the feature for which the island as a whole was originally named: the Gaelic word 'Mull' translates as 'mass of hill'. The western coast of the island is especially attractive. Rare orchids, irises and other plant species grow here in abundance, colonies of nesting guillemots crowd its cliffs and its hidden inlets are a haven for families of seals.

Gylen Castle
ISLE OF KERRERA

Next page. The MacDougalls built this impressive castle in 1582, but it was burnt down by Sir James Leslie's Covenanters in 1642. So called because, in 1638, they had signed a 'National Covenant' refusing to compromise their Presbyterian beliefs and practices as England's King Charles I had demanded, the Covenanters fought bravely for religious freedom. The English king's interference had been resented both on nationalistic and religious grounds: soon, of course, his own country's puritans would tire of his high church sympathies and dictatorial ways.

Kiloran Bay
ISLE OF COLONSAY

Right. Atlantic rollers pound the sand of this most beautiful of sandy beaches. The tropic blue of the sea should not be too surprising. The Gulf Stream washes the Hebrides, and if it carries with it abundant moisture to fall as rain, it also brings balmy warmth to this improbable riviera of the north. It brings other things too, notably nickernut seed pods fallen from trees in the Caribbean and borne here by the current. These were once worn as good-luck charms by the islanders, who sensed their exoticism.

Portnahaven
ISLE OF ISLAY

Next page. "Very good for fishing, inhabited and manured" noted Dean Monro approvingly on his visit to this Islay village in 1549. Portnahaven has grown little in the centuries since, but it still presents an impression of prosaic industry and orderliness that even a sunny island day cannot set aside. The local fishery has declined; instead, Portnahaven has become the centre for a new industry that could grow inestimably in importance in the years to come: the wave-powered generation of electricity.

Kilnave Chapel and Cross
LOCH GRUINART, ISLE OF ISLAY

Right. A badly damaged Celtic cross stands beside the ruined chapel at Kilnave, while the grey waters of Loch Gruinart lap the shore nearby. All in all, a fittingly desolate scene for a hideous crime, committed four centuries ago in the vicious clan warfare of 1598. A group of fleeing MacLeans, it is said, took refuge here from the MacDonalds. Unimpressed by the fact that their foes had sought sanctuary in a hallowed place, their pursuers simply set the chapel on fire and burned them alive.

Distillery
LAGAVULIN, ISLE OF ISLAY

Next page. Scotch whisky is famous the world over: there are scores of single malts on sale, but for many conoisseurs the finest come from Islay. There are fashions in these things, and recently it seems that the Islay malts are in vogue to the extent that Lagavulin whisky has had to be rationed. The distilleries at Ardbeg, Bowmore, Caol Ila and Port Ellen are doing just as well. The secret lies in the 'peaty' quality of these whiskies: the malt for them is smoked over peat-burning fires.

Towards Ardminish
ISLE OF GIGHA

Right. "Out of the world and into Gigha" goes a saying still heard in the west sometimes, and this small island off the coast of Kintyre feels different even by Hebridean standards. Yet it is one of the most accessible of the islands; thousands flock here every year to enjoy the famous Achamore Gardens at Gigha's southern end. The botanical extravaganza contrived here highlights the peculiar advantages of the Hebridean climate: the warm waters of the Gulf Stream ensure that it never gets really cold.

Rothesay Harbour
ISLE OF BUTE

Next page. Rothesay has been a haven for coastal shipping for at least a thousand years. It was officially declared a 'royal burgh' in 1401. This was historically significant in ensuring that Bute stayed firmly in the Scottish sphere of influence, rather than in that of the Lordship of the Isles. The bustling harbour, long a landing-place for fish, is now a popular port of call for pleasure craft – so much so that Rothesay has (quite unfairly) gained a reputation as a tourist trap.

Grampians and Aberdeen

It is extraordinary how attitudes and understandings change: "To the southern inhabitants of Scotland", wrote Dr Johnson in the 1770s, "the state of the mountains and the islands is equally unknown with that of Borneo and Sumatra."

To the English, of course, these lands seemed still more remote – and with none of the enticing exoticism Johnson's comparison suggests. To them the Highlands were a wasteland; quite literally a waste of land. With the nineteenth century, however, came a shift in sensibility. In the age of Romanticism, bleak was beautiful, and the more wild and rugged the

scenery the better. The poems and novels of Sir Walter Scott at once responded to and helped mould this change of taste. The fashion found an influential patron in Her Majesty, Queen Victoria, who had her own castle built at Balmoral, on what now became 'Royal Deeside'.

The royal connection continues, and still draws many thousands of sightseers to the region each year, though people also come to walk, climb, bike and birdwatch – and simply to enjoy the rugged grandeur of the Grampians. In fact, there is no sign whatsoever of the mountains going out of fashion: new visitors are discovering its beauties every year.

Elgin Cathedral
MORAYSHIRE

Right. The Reformation was the defining moment in Scottish history. The country changed, abruptly and for ever, in 1560. Elgin's fine medieval cathedral, renowned as the 'Lantern of the North', suddenly found itself without a function. Except, of course, as a quarry of ready-dressed building stone (the gothic rood-screen was chopped up for firewood). In more modern times, the pieties of heritage concern have come to the cathedral's rescue and the building has belatedly been preserved. But it is hard to regret its ruined state: to stroll here – especially at twilight – is to experience a uniquely haunting atmosphere.

Tormore Distillery
SPEYSIDE, GRAMPIAN

Next page. Just over a mile west of Ballindalloch, Strathspey, the Tormore distillery was established in 1958 – the first new distillery to be built in the Highlands for sixty years. A risky step, perhaps, but it turned out to have been a triumph: Tormore has been one of the most sought-after malts in recent years. Sir Albert Richardson designed the distillery in a spirit of elegance and fun. The grounds boast ornamental fountains and a lake, while the main building has attractive dormer windows and a tiny belfry.

Buchan Ness Lighthouse
BODDAM, ABERDEENSHIRE

Right. Standing at Boddam, the Buchan Ness was built in 1827. It was designed by Robert Stevenson, grandfather of the famous novelist (who would eventually help him edit his memoir of an engineering life). Equipped with a flashing light, the first in Scotland, the new light was crucial given the mounting significance of the fishing port of Peterhead to the north. There was also a growing traffic of vessels to and from Boddam itself, including heavy carriers for the pink granite for which the area was becoming famed.

Stonehaven Harbour
ABERDEENSHIRE

Next page. "Stonehive" wrote one eighteenth-century traveller, was "a little fishing town, remarkable for nothing but its harbour." Today that judgement seems a little harsh. But, as night falls on the British fishing industry, and North Sea oil production too appears to have passed its zenith, communities all along Scotland's eastern coast are facing challenges. There are good grounds for hope, however: these towns have weathered many a storm in the past, and there is every reason to suppose that they will weather many more.

Dunnottar Castle
STONEHAVEN, ABERDEENSHIRE

Right. The morning sunshine on Dunnottar Castle, an impressive ruin south of Stonehaven in the heart of the coastal strip known as 'the Mearns'. The Gaelic name *Dunnottar* means 'the castle on the point' and that description still largely sums up the place today. Irish sources state that there was a fort here from about AD 680; it is known to have been besieged by Vikings in the AD 890s, but the present structure dates from the twelfth to fifteenth centuries.

Slains Castle
CRUDEN, ABERDEENSHIRE

Next page. Much (and ineptly) modified since its first construction in the early seventeenth century, Slains is neither the most attractive nor the most authentic of Scotland's castles. But you would have to go a long way to find one that was more atmospheric than this gaunt ruin that seems to teeter atop a giddy cliff just north of Cruden, Aberdeenshire. Bram Stoker was inspired by Slains to write his story of *Dracula* (1897), which features "a vast ruined castle, from whose windows came no ray of light".

Craigievar Castle
ALFORD, ABERDEENSHIRE

Right. This famous pile outside Alford, Aberdeenshire, was built more for show than for military substance if the truth be told. Its original owner, William Forbes, was a merchant in the Baltic trade, and he had the castle built in 1610–18. Its magnificence can hardly be disputed, though, and it has been beautifully looked after since being built, with the result that many of its original Jacobean fittings still remain. It is now in the care of the National Trust for Scotland.

Brig o'Dee
ABERDEEN

Next page. The old Brig o'Dee, outside Braemar, was built by military engineers in the eighteenth century, when the Hanoverians were desperate to suppress the Jacobite spirit once and for all. Queen Victoria was as aware as anyone of the irony that this sometime hotbed of sedition should have been reinvented in her reign as 'Royal Deeside'. She loved the romance of Jacobitism, in fact, like just about everybody else at the time, even if she never took its claims to a Stewart succession seriously.

Central Scotland

All the romance – and many of the contradictions – of Scotland is summed up in the figure of 'Rob Roy' MacGregor. A real person, he was born near Loch Katrine in 1671, but he was also a fictional character – most famously in Sir Walter Scott's novel of 1818, though his legend was well-established by that time.

If Rob Roy's historical status is ambiguous, so too was his moral nature, as he lived both within and outside the law. The true-life MacGregor (who, typically, confused things by calling himself 'Campbell' in honour of his mother) was the quite legitimate owner of extensive lands to the east of Loch Lomond. Yet he was simultaneously a brigand, raiding

Lowland farms with his men and stealing cattle, or extorting money in a form of protection rackets. He was not officially outlawed until after the Jacobite rebellion of 1715, in which he had (apparently reluctantly) participated in the Stewart cause.

An unlikely icon? Not in English eyes, in which Scotland is still at once stirringly wild but fundamentally friendly; nor in the context of a Scotland that even today has mixed feelings about the Union. It is hard to resist reading that ambivalence into the landscape of Central Scotland: romantic, un-English, but essentially beautiful and benign.

City Centre
DUNDEE

Right. Like many another British city, Dundee has suffered at the hands of the post-war planners, with large swathes of the urban fabric being sliced away for major road schemes or retail developments. In the streets around its centre, though, the visitor still gets a very vivid sense of the bustling, pleasant place this used to be. Handsome rather than pretty, perhaps; even a little 'dour' in the stereotypically Scottish way, but incontrovertibly attractive – and with a majestic setting beside the Firth of Tay.

Panorama
DUNDEE

Next page. 'Jute, Jam and Journalism' was famously the formula for Dundee's prosperity, though the city had first come to prominence as centre for the whaling industry. None of these trades was destined to survive the twentieth century intact, though a downsized D.C. 'Beano' Thomson still has a presence. Of more significance now is the university, whose tower by the Tay can be seen here. Along with a major teaching hospital and a science park on the outskirts, this is enabling the city to move forward into a high-tech future.

Birch Trees
ABERFELDY, PERTHSHIRE

Right. "Come, let us spend the lightsome days / In the birks of Aberfeldie!" Robert Burns' amorous invitation put Aberfeldy on the tourist map 200 years ago, and Dorothy Wordsworth was just one of a throng of eager visitors roaming up and down the valley, attempting to identify which particular *birks* (birch trees) Scotland's national bard had had in mind. There is really no way of knowing, but local tradition proposes this beauty spot by the River Tay: it is indeed a wonderfully romantic setting.

Drummond Castle Gardens
CRIEFF, PERTHSHIRE

Next page. Dating from the fifteenth century, Drummond Castle, outside Crieff, is handsome enough, but it is comprehensively upstaged by its spectacular gardens. These were laid out in the seventeenth century in the extravagant Baroque style of the day, the designers paying particular attention to French and Italian models. This is hyper-horticulture, the garden at its farthest imaginable remove from nature. The total effect is magnificent, even mesmerizing, yet profoundly 'un-Scottish' too, it might be felt, by those for whom a certain romantic wildness is the vital key to Caledonian beauty.

Kinnoull Tower
KINNOULL HILL, PERTHSHIRE

Right. A little glimpse of the Rhineland in the Tay Valley, Kinnoull Tower perches atop a rugged outcrop a few miles east of Perth, the stone-built souvenir of an aristocrat's continental holiday. A folly it may be, but it is a glorious one: it dominates the landscape for miles up and down the valley. And its conception was not entirely whimsical. The ninth Earl of Kinnoull, who had the tower built in the eighteenth century, seems to have seen it as a job-creation scheme in a difficult economic time.

Towards Loch Rannoch and Schiehallion
PERTHSHIRE

Next page. One of Scotland's most distinctive mountains is seen here reflected in the waters of Loch Rannoch to entrancing effect, but there has always been an air of enchantment about Schiehallion. The Gaelic name, *Sìdh Chaillean*, means 'Fairy Hill of the Caledonians', and few visitors are able to resist its magic. It is ironic, in the circumstances, that scientists Nevil Maskelyne and John Playfair should in 1774 have used the slopes of Schiehallion for the least mystical of purposes: that of estimating the mass of planet Earth.

Robert the Bruce Statue
BANNOCKBURN, STIRLING

Right. The mounted figure of Robert I, 'The Bruce', dominates the field at Bannockburn, outside Stirling, just as it did on that fateful day in 1314. On that day, the Scottish King led from the front, guiding his force to an historic victory over the much larger army of England's Edward II. Comparable triumphs would be in short supply over the centuries that followed. Despite this – and despite the Union of 1707 – patriotic fervour still runs high, and Scots of every political hue take pride in the achievement of Bannockburn.

Stirling Bridge
STIRLING

Next page. The bridge we see today was built later – probably downstream of its medieval predecessor – but it is still a stirring sight for any Scot. For it was at the Battle of Stirling Bridge that, on 11 September 1297, William Wallace won a famous victory over English might. Wallace's army was massively outnumbered, but this hardly mattered on the narrow bridge: anything up to 20,000 English were killed as they tried to force their way across. Wallace's exploits were commemorated in stone in the nineteenth century when a tower-monument was built on a nearby hill.

ROBERT
THE
BRUCE
KING

Stirling Castle
STIRLING

Right. *Striveling*, 'place of strife', seems to have been Stirling's original Anglo-Saxon name, and it could hardly have been more appropriate for a fortress-town which controlled the main route to the north. William Wallace defeated the English at Stirling Bridge in 1297, taking the castle for the Scots; the field of Bannockburn is just a few miles away. The castle was fought over again in the seventeenth century when General Monck captured it for Cromwell, and again in the eighteenth, when Bonnie Prince Charlie tried, but failed, to take it.

The Lake of Menteith
STIRLING

Next page. Definitely a 'lake' rather than a 'loch', this is the only stretch of water so-called in Scotland. Scholars suggest that this anomaly may result from confusion over the use of the Gaelic word *laigh* meaning 'low ground'. But by any name, this is a spellbinding place, especially when, as here, a silent dawn tinges the sky above the Trossachs. On an island in the lake stand the ruins of the old Augustinian priory of Inchmahome, founded by Walter Comyn in 1238.

Edinburgh, Lothian and Fife

Today Edinburgh is famous the world over for its festivals. Every aspect of the arts and media is celebrated here. Though the top performers in music, theatre and other artistic fields flock each year to the official International Festival, the so-called 'Fringe Festival' has in some ways surpassed it in significance.

Add to this important film and TV events, plus the world's most successful International Book Festival and it becomes clear why the Edinburgh 'brand' is acknowledged everywhere. But then Scotland has always been an outward-looking country, with the Scots seeing themselves as citizens of a wider world. At times this has been a matter

of strategy: from Mary, Queen of Scots to Bonnie Prince Charlie, Scots leaders have hoped that contacts 'across the water' would help them outflank England.

There is much more to it than anti-Englishness, though. The old kingdom of Scotland was very much a maritime nation, its trade with the Baltic a key to its prosperity. From Leith, Dunfermline and a host of now-forgotten ports in Fife and the Firth of Forth, close relations with the Continent were maintained. Today that traffic has declined, but the cultural commerce has continued: this region has become Scotland's window on the world.

Tantallon Castle
EAST LOTHIAN

Right. Dramatically sited on its coastal clifftop, Tantallon Castle was built by the Douglas family around 1375. A curtain wall 3.6 m (12 ft) thick cut this little headland off from the landward side, while safe within rose a round keep six storeys high. The Douglases' regular fallings out with one another and with their kings ensured that the castle saw plenty of action in the fifteenth and sixteenth centuries. In 1651 Cromwell's General Monck subjected it to a twelve-day bombardment, effectively reducing it to ruins.

Towards Edinburgh Castle
PRINCES STREET GARDENS, EDINBURGH

Next page. The ancient British writer Gildas, writing 1,500 years ago, tells us that the Celtic Goddodin tribe had a hilltop fort at 'Etyn'. The castle on its rocky outcrop dominates Edinburgh to this day. For centuries, however, it would not have been seen from this exact angle, as the present-day Princes Street Gardens were originally under water. Not until 1763 was the Nor' Loch drained, clearing the way for the construction of a more spacious and elegant New Town, of which Princes Street itself would mark the southern edge.

Edinburgh Castle and St Cuthbert's
EDINBURGH

Right. Above the trees can be seen the shapely spire of St Cuthbert's, its leafy churchyard a peaceful refuge from the noise and bustle of Princes Street. Beyond rises the mass of the Castle Rock, what remains of an extinct volcano, with the castle buildings clustered round the top. The oldest, St Margaret's Chapel, dates from the eleventh century. Every day except Sunday a gun is fired from the battlements at one o'clock in the afternoon. Originally this was done so ships in Leith Harbour could check their chronometers.

Edinburgh Military Tattoo
EDINBURGH

Next page. The world beats its path to Scotland's door each summer to take part in that great extravaganza that is the Edinburgh Festival: three weeks of fun and culture, high and low. There is film, theatre, opera, music of every description, book events and stand-up comedy. And then, of course, there is the celebrated Tattoo. After all the excitement and colour of the military bands, stunt-teams and dancing troupes from all over the world, the evening ends on a more melancholy note with the lament of the lone piper in the castle turret.

Towards Linlithgow Palace
LINLITHGOW LOCH, WEST LOTHIAN

Right. A winter sun shines on the Palace of Linlithgow, viewed across the icy waters of Linlithgow Loch. Mary, Queen of Scots was born here in 1542, and her unhappy story still seems to haunt the place. Her deposition from the throne, her flight into England and her imprisonment and eventual execution there on Elizabeth's orders, would certainly bring bad fortune to Linlithgow. No longer a royal residence, it never really thrived under the Anglo-Scottish Union, and remains today a small West Lothian town.

Hopetoun House
WEST LOTHIAN

Next page. This was an ordinary West Lothian mansion when it was built for the Hope family at the end of the seventeenth century. By 1730, however, the family had been ennobled. After this, something statelier seemed to be called for, so the new Earl of Hopetoun brought in William Adam, and over several years first he and then his sons John and Robert went to work. They re-created the house along its present, positively palatial lines: it has been described, not altogether fancifully, as a Scottish Versailles.

Forth Rail Bridge
NORTH QUEENSFERRY, FIFE

Right. This miracle of Victorian engineering, instantly recognizable the world over, celebrated its centenary in 1990. It was designed by John Fowler and Benjamin Baker and built by William Arrol. It joins North Queensferry, Fife (pictured) with South Queensferry on the Lothian side. As their names suggest, a ferry used to ply between these points. The 'queen' concerned was the eleventh-century monarch Margaret, whose son David I ordered monks to establish a service here. A suspension bridge for road traffic was opened in 1964.

Anstruther Harbour
EAST NEUK, FIFE

Next page. Anstruther lies in the picturesque East Neuk of Fife, one of the loveliest – and least known – corners of Scotland. The secret is getting out, though: tourists are coming here in increased numbers, and pleasure craft are beginning to outnumber fishing boats in the harbour. The size of its harbour hints at the importance Anstruther once had, not just for its fishery, but as a port for continental trade. The herring fishery remained crucial, though, and whilst that has declined in recent years, Anstruther is home to the Scottish Fisheries Museum.

St Andrew's Cathedral
ST ANDREWS, FIFE

Right. Looking along what would have been the main aisle of St Andrew's Cathedral from west to east, the visitor cannot help being overwhelmed by its stupendous scale. It seems still more surprising given the tiny size of the city now, and its remoteness from the modern beaten track. In medieval times, however, this was one of the great pilgrimage sites of Europe, on a par with England's Canterbury Cathedral and Santiago de Compostela, Spain. People came from all over Christendom to worship at the Apostle's shrine.

St Andrew's Cathedral and Town
FIFE

Next page. The view from St Rule's Tower, St Andrews shows the edge of the Cathedral precincts, and the streets of the university city itself. Prince William, Britain's future king, began studying here in 2001. Although St Andrews' academic excellence and venerable history were no doubt points in its favour, there can be little doubt that, for those charged with the Prince's security, the sheer isolation of this tiny city must have been a recommendation, situated as it is far out on the northeastern coast of Fife.

Glasgow, Clyde Valley and Argyll

Scotland is too often seen in stereotypes. Some, having heard much of its wild beauty, are surprised to find it has any towns at all. Others, brought up on the tough TV cop Taggart, or on the spiky realism of Irvine Welsh's *Trainspotting*, are more or less unaware of the existence of scenic Scotland.

No region has suffered more from such stereotyping than the west of Scotland, wrongly assumed to be a single, continuous urban sprawl. Granted, Glasgow is the centre of a major modern conurbation, parts of which are not exactly easy on the eye, but there is a great deal more to the region than brick and concrete.

Across much of the region exist scenes of post-industrial dereliction: rusting gantries, abandoned gasholders and dilapidated factories. These, ironically, were once held to represent a heroic future for Scotland; already, it appears, they are monuments to the past. Their failure has meant misery for thousands, but the hope is that new economic opportunities will be found – ones which do not leave such unsightly scars on the Scottish landscape. For, despite the stereotypes, this is still an overwhelmingly lovely part of the world, which must be preserved for future generations.

Burial Cairn
KILMARTIN, ARGYLL

Right. As the crow flies, the great city of Glasgow lies less than 40 miles from here, but the roar of urban life never seemed so far away. And yet, from perhaps 9,000 years ago, there seems to have been something of a prehistoric metropolis around what is now the village of Kilmartin in Argyll. Some, like the Nether Largie Cairns, shown here, are clearly burial sites, but there are also standing stones and other, unidentified, remains, dating from the Stone Age through to the Pictish period.

Towards Castle Stalker
APPIN, ARGYLL

Next page. Castle Stalker takes centre-stage in this majestic Appin panorama, with the Morvern Hills behind and the waters of Loch Laich before. Built in the fifteenth century, the castle fell into ruins soon after, only to be recommissioned in the eighteenth century by the Crown. Across Europe, the advent of the modern era had rendered castles obsolete: even in Scotland, this had been the case. But, with a series of Jacobite rebellions making much of the Highlands ungovernable, there was a clear role for strongholds such as this.

Ben Cruachan

ARGYLL

Right. This is a land for all seasons. Every time of year has its special quality, and it is impossible to decide which displays the Scottish scenery to its best advantage. Here we can see the first touch of Winter frost on the ground and trees as we look across to Ben Cruachan from East Argyll. The early morning sun dispells some of the chill in the upland air. Nearby the river Orchy flows into Loch Awe, whose waters in their turn find their way down the Pass of Brander to Loch Etive.

Sunset

OBAN BAY, ARGYLL

Next page. Oban Bay lies ashimmer beneath the wonderful colours of a setting sun, with the dark outline of Kerrera beyond. A jewel in its own right and known for the ruined Gylen Castle, this little island has the important secondary function of providing a natural breakwater for Oban. Savage storms lash this coast each year tearing up the Firth of Lorne, but Kerrera and the Isles of Mull bear the brunt allowing Oban a sheltered anchorage.

Loch Fyne
ARGYLL

Right. Winter reflections upon Loch Fyne highlight wispy clouds and a grey-silk sky endowing Glen Kinglas with a distinctly ethereal air. At the head of the glen rises Ben Ime, but there is access to Glen Croe via the famous pass known as 'Rest and Be Thankful'. That name was inscribed beside a grassy bench left there by General Wade's engineers who built a road here in the eighteenth century. The new military roads helped open up the Highlands economically, though drovers disliked their narrow tracks and hard metalled surfaces.

Barcaldine Castle
BENDERLOCH, ARGYLL

Next page. Built in the early years of the sixteenth century, Barcaldine Castle, Benderloch, is often known as the 'Black Castle', supposedly on account of the dark colour of its stones. In this exquisite Summer scene, however, the sun illuminates everything from the grassy tussocks in the foreground to the just discernible hills of Appin on the far horizon. In the middle distance can just be seen the grey waters of Loch Creran. Barcaldine commanded the entrance to this strategically important sea loch.

Strathaven Church
LANARKSHIRE

Right. Strathaven (or 'Stra'ven' as it is known) is a handsome little Lanarkshire town. Its origins are medieval, but it clearly came of age in the eighteenth century, when it emerged as a thriving centre for textiles, especially cotton. The East Parish church spire is the most recongisable landmark in the town, stetching high above any of the other buildings. It was built in 1777 and is one of three Church of Scotland parishes in the close-knit, religious community.

Gourock
FIRTH OF CLYDE

Next page. Warm sunshine lights up the little town of Gourock and the Firth of Clyde, the coast of Cowal visible across the water. Gourock's fortunes have always been to some extent tied to those of the region to westward – a ferry has plied from here to Dunoon since the seventeenth century. By the late nineteenth century, a rail-link to Glasgow had enabled it to establish itself as something of a tourist hub, offering steamship cruises to all the major destinations on the Firth of Clyde.

George Square
GLASGOW

Right. James Watt had the inspiration for his steam condenser when he was walking across Glasgow Green in 1764, and it earned him this statue in George Square. Glasgow had been a thriving merchant city and seat of learning for generations before the Industrial Revolution, but engineering was undoubtedly the making of the modern city. Steel, shipbuilding and other heavy industries made this the 'second city of the Empire' for a time, but it has struggled to find an economic identity in the post-industrial age.

George Square
GLASGOW

Next page. Built in the 1880s, and opened by Queen Victoria, the City Chambers gave Glasgow's George Square an impressively finished feel. Some smaller buildings would be added later, but once this magnificent structure was in place, the city had a civic centre it could be proud of. Sumptuously decorated within, it is a monument not just to the architecture but to the municipal values of the Victorian age. Elegant offices, a majestic council chamber and imposing committee rooms testify to the seriousness with which nineteenth-century Glasgow took the business of local government.

River Kelvin
KELVINGROVE PARK, GLASGOW

Right. To walk beside the River Kelvin on an afternoon in summer is quickly to forget the busy city so close at hand. Above the trees beyond the weir appears the spire of the university, which was originally established in 1451. The great Victorian building boom has left us with a false impression of Glasgow, and it is a much more venerable place than is generally assumed. It was founded in the sixth century, and its cathedral dates from the thirteenth: it was old before the first steam-hammer was ever built.

Kelvingrove
GLASGOW

Next page. Dusk lends a certain drama to the scene in Glasgow's West End. Kelvingrove Park is in the foreground, with the last remaining sun illuminating the elegant façade of the Art Gallery and Museum. The gallery houses one of Britain's most important art collections, with works by internationally revered Old Masters and Impressionists as well as by the important figures of Scottish art. The West End might be described as Glasgow's 'Latin Quarter', bustling with academic, intellectual and cultural life.

South-West Scotland

Scotland's southwestern counties have remained almost entirely unknown to outsiders, despite perhaps being the country's most accessible part. Just across the border from Carlisle the main road northward takes the traveller through a region of lovely, if understated, scenery, with towns and villages as pretty as any in the British Isles.

That is the point, of course: this has always been a region that wayfarers passed through on their way to the cities of the Central Lowlands and beyond. As for Galloway and Ayrshire, lying farther westward, these have to a large extent been by-passed by modern

tourism as surely as they were by-passed by so much of modern history. Had it not been for the road (and, until the 1960s, the railway) to Stranraer, and the ferry from there to Ireland, it seems reasonable to wonder whether any outsider would have come this way at all.

Even now, the vagaries of the transmitter system mean many here have to watch Northern Irish television – the south-west is in some ways semi-detached from the rest of Scotland. Yet it is also one of the most beautiful areas of the country, with a fascinating history and a very special character all of its own.

Ayr

AYRSHIRE

Right. Long a prosperous market town, by the 1780s Ayr was a significant port, with some 300 vessels calling every year. Add in the growing tourist trade, helped on by Ayr's association with that great romantic icon, Robert Burns, and it can be imagined how heady the mood was here in the nineteenth cntury. Ayr was, according to Robert Chambers, "a handsome town in a flourishing condition." Handsome it remains, if not quite flourishing, but Ayr is a considerable place, with much to offer the visitor even now.

Wellington Square

AYR, AYRSHIRE

Next page. The size and splendour of the town courthouse, the County Buildings, seen here across the spacious flowerbeds of Wellington Square, announce the extent of Ayr's aspirations when it was built in 1823. It was constructed as part of a major remodelling closely based on Edinburgh's acclaimed New Town, and comparisons with the capital were routine. Ayr became a place of fashion, even boasting its own school for "young ladies of quality"; one Victorian visitor described it as "a provincial capital of considerable social standing".

Burns Monument
ALLOWAY, AYRSHIRE

Right. The single arch of the 'Auld Brig o'Doon', from where this photo was taken, was "the largest I ever saw" according to Daniel Defoe, but this little settlement just south of Ayr would soon have a far greater claim to fame. In 1759, Robert Burns, destined to become Scotland's national bard, was born here into a poor farming family. His monument seems over-stately for a natural rebel with radical views (and sometimes wayward morals) – but then there was part of him that always yearned for respectable acceptance.

Dunure Castle
HEADS OF AYR, AYRSHIRE

Next page. Mary, Queen of Scots saw this dramatic coastline when she stayed in nearby Dunure Castle in the course of a royal progress of 1563. Just a few years later Gilbert Kennedy, Earl of Cassilis, would prove a far less genial host when he roasted a certain Allan Stewart on a spit. The Commendator of Crossraguel Abbey, Stewart had refused to hand over abbey lands which Kennedy had long coveted for himself. Today the castle is a ruin, almost indistinguishable from the rocks of the coast.

Drumlanrig Castle
DUMFRIES AND GALLOWAY

Right. Two earlier fortresses stood on this site, but Drumlanrig is a castle in name only – call it what you like, though, it is an extremely impressive pile. Built late in the seventeenth century for the 1st Duke of Queensberry, it is a fine example of the baroque style – extravagantly ornate in its detail and yet in overall impression beautifully restrained. And the house itself is just the start: standing at the centre of a 48,000-hectare (120,000-acre) estate, Drumlanrig has spacious parkland and some of Scotland's most celebrated ornamental gardens.

Caerlaverock Castle
SOLWAY FIRTH, DUMFRIES-SHIRE

Next page. The visitor's first impression of Caerlaverock Castle is that half of it must have been razed by the forces of Edward I who besieged it in 1300, or blown up by the Covenanters who captured it in 1640. Only then does it sink in that the present structure, dating from 1425, though a ruin, is remarkably well-preserved but built to a highly unorthodox triangular design. It still cuts an impressive figure on its site above the salt marshes of the Solway Firth.

Gatehouse of Fleet
KIRKCUDBRIGHTSHIRE

Right. Gatehouse of Fleet was made – and arguably saved – by paternalism. The town as we see it was built in the eighteenth century, James Murray of Cally planning the whole place, with tannery, textile works and other places of manufacture, all driven by water mills. The nineteenth century saw a slow decline and then with the twentieth came tourism which, seizing on such a delightful spot, seemed set to destroy it. But Mrs Murray Usher, James's descendant, set strict controls on new development, so preserving one of Scotland's most attractive towns.

Bruce's Stone
GLENTROOL, GALLOWAY

Next page. Not a prehistoric megalith, this monument was raised in 1929 in commemoration of the Battle of Glentrool. In 1307, the miserably depleted force of the all but defeated Robert the Bruce gained an unexpected triumph over a substantial English army. They employed guerrilla tactics, hiding out in these wooded ravines and then toppling boulders down upon the enemy column. It is appropriate, then, that his memorial takes this form, on the hillside above Loch Trool in what is now part of the Galloway Forest Park.

Borders

The 'Debatable Land', strictly speaking, lay to the west of the present Borders region, the area lying between the Rivers Esk and Sark. This area was claimed by both Scotland and England for several centuries before it was finally divided up in 1552. But this controversial scrap of land is often taken as emblematic of the Borders as a whole, its character formed in uncertainty and violence.

This was a wild frontier and the culture of the Border reivers really existed, even if its romance may have been concocted by later balladeers and writers. Although tradition may

have exaggerated the heroism of their activities, tending to characterize them as 'raids', it has also given a misleading sense of their true scale. Low-level raiding was indeed a way of life on both sides of the border, the English often raiding English neighbours and the Scots attacking their fellow Scots. As well as countless minor forays back and forth, there were also large-scale expeditions, some Scottish campaigns reaching as far south as York.

Fiercely fought over for hundreds of years, this was a country whose ownership may have been up for grabs, but whose sense of Scottishness was only strengthened by that fact.

Suspension Bridge
PEEBLES, PEEBLESHIRE

Right. A suspension bridge spans the River Tweed at Peebles, one of the prettiest towns in the Borders, historically a textiles town but now most famous for its Hydro. This luxury hotel opened in 1881, and its effect was to make the town a genteel and prosperous inland resort, visitors flocking here for fresh air, fishing, bathing and walking, and for touring farther afield through the Border region. The formula was to prove a winning one: the Hydro has continued to thrive, its bookings boosted by a growing conference trade.

Sir Walter Scott's House
ABBOTSFORD, NEAR GALASHIELS

Next page. It would not be much of an exaggeration to say that Sir Walter Scott reinvented Scotland for Victorian Britain – and for the world: a country of kilted clansmen, bonnie lassies and romantic bards. Readers from France to Russia devoured his poems and the best-selling novels that brought him not just fame but a considerable fortune. Abbotsford was his hobby: he built a villa here in 1811, but it grew and grew. He filled it with over 9,000 books and all manner of curiosities from Scottish history – a field which he had very much made his own.

River Tweed

LADYKIRK, BERWICKSHIRE

Right. Beyond the river lies England: the frontier follows the meandering course of the lower Tweed before striking off southward into the Cheviot Hills a few miles west of here. Before the bridge was built at Berwick at the end of the thirteenth century, two fords near here were the only easy way across the river and, for several hundred hectic years in the Middle Ages, invasion forces practically commuted back and forth across these shallows. The bridge here was not built until 1901.

St Abbs

BERWICKSHIRE

Next page. The clifftop walks along the coast around St Abbs are some of the loveliest in the country – though in a brisk east wind it can be a rather bracing experience! Full of hidden creeks and inlets, its rocks are a navigational nightmare for outsiders; this coast was a centre for smuggling in the eighteenth century. It was not just the obvious luxuries that were imported illicitly: wool and hides were both brought in from the Continent as contraband to escape protectionist tariffs levied by the Crown.

Sir Walter Scott's Tomb

DRYBURGH ABBEY, ROXBURGHSHIRE

Right. Amid the ruins of this twelfth-century abbey lie the mortal remains of Sir Walter Scott, for better or worse the inventor of Shortbread Scotland. His impact in works like *Marmion* (1808), *Waverley* (1814) and *The Heart of Midlothian* (1818) can scarcely be overestimated: his stirring stories created Caledoniamania not just in Britain but beyond. Easy as it is to sneer – and his Scotland does seem terribly sentimentalized now – he put the country on the imaginative map for readers around the world.

Countryside

KELSO, ROXBURGHSHIRE

Next page. The rolling country around Kelso could hardly be more peaceful now, but invaders trampled these green fields in days gone by. The Earl of Hertford's men slaughtered the monks of the nearby abbey in 1545, just one entry in a catalogue of killing. The accession of James VI of Scotland to the English throne as James I in 1603 drew the sting from an enmity which was officially abolished with the Act of Union of 1707. But the rivalries – and sometimes the resentments – linger on.

Kelso Abbey
KELSO, ROXBURGHSHIRE

Right. Kelso's monastic community survived the destruction of the Abbey buildings in 1545, essentially camping out in appropriated churches and other buildings. With the Reformation, however, it was suppressed once and for all. The impact on Kelso was considerable – a medieval monastery is not just a spiritual centre but an economic hub – but it managed to make its way as a market town. As time went on, its inhabitants built successful brewing and linen-bleaching trades; now of course it has a thriving tourist trade.

Acknowledgements

Biography

Michael Kerrigan lives in Edinburgh, where he writes regularly for the *Scotsman* newspaper. He is a book reviewer for *The Times Literary Supplement* and the *Guardian*, London. As an author, he has published extensively on both British and world history and prehistory. He has been a contributor to Flame Tree's *World History* and *Irish History* as well as to *The Times Encyclopaedia of World Religion* (2001).

Picture Credits

Courtesy of iStock (www.istockphoto.com) and the following: BMPix 22–23, 45; theasis 25, 83, 125, 161; Chalky White 26–27; Lucentius 30–31, 79; spumador 33; Johnbraid 41; Hanskwaspen 49; fotoVoyager 54–55; NicolasMcComber 57; Munro1 149; Rkotulan 68–69; generacionx 71; jubraun11 76–77; philzero 80–81; abzee 87, 130–31, 134–35; kyrien 93; manu10319 94–95; elgol 98–99, 105; trotalo 101; Norimack 118–119; DouglasMcGilviray 133; Gannet77 137; Rae_The_Sparrow 145; Aarstudio 157; antb 170–71; Travel Library Limited 173; Empato 177; northlightimages 181; Gim42 182–83; jentakespictures 185; Hpuschmann 186–187; Derek McDougall 197, 201, 206–07; JuliScalzi 198–99; JohnFScott 213, 234–35; DevelopingPerceptions 214–15; Roll6 241; Khrizmo 245; Gannet77 249.

Courtesy of Superstock (www.superstock.com) and the following: Weber Raphael/Prisma 21; Melba/age fotostock 29; Ian Murray/age fotostock 34–35; Douglas Houghton/age fotostock 42–43; Prisma 46–47; Pearl Bucknall/Loop Images 53; Vidler Steve/Prisma 67; Nadia Isakova/Jon Arnold Images 84–85; Sebastian Wasek/age fotostock 106–107; Design Pics 109, 117; Edmund Nägele/Mauritius 113; Nomad 126–27; Gerth Roland/Prisma 129; Tim Graham/ Robert Harding Picture Library 138–39; Mauritius 150–151; Travel Library Limited 162–63; age fotostock 169; Travel Pictures Ltd 174–75; Robert Harding Picture Library 193, 194–95, 233; Eye Ubiquitous 209; Findlay Rankin/age fotostock 226–27; Ivan Vdovin/age fotostock 229; Cultura Limited 246–47.

Courtesy of Getty (www.gettyimages.co.uk) and the following: Foto Voyager 50–51; Visit Britain and Britain on View 58–59, 221, 242–43; Alf Thomas 110–11; Roger Coulam 61; Kit Downey Photography 178–79; PremiumUIG 202–03; Dawahar images 205; Nikki Bidgood 210–11; Dennis Barnes 222–23, 225; James Ross 250–51.

Courtesy of Shutterstock (www.shuterstock.com) and the following: Steve Horsley 72–73; John A Cemeron 75, 102–103, 154–55; duchy 97; Jaime Pharr 114–115; Lisa A 146–47; godrick 153; Avresa 158–59; Kevin Eaves 230–31; PHB.cz (Richard Semik) 253.

Index